The Little
SPICE
Cookbook

THE LITTLE
SPICE
COOKBOOK

ULTIMATE
EDITIONS

Publisher Joanna Lorenz
Senior Cookery Editor Linda Fraser
Assistant Editor Emma Brown
Copy Editor Jenni Fleetwood
Designer Lilian Lindblom
Illustrator Anna Koska

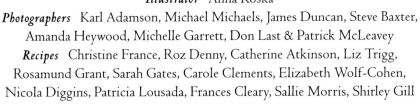

Photographers Karl Adamson, Michael Michaels, James Duncan, Steve Baxter,
Amanda Heywood, Michelle Garrett, Don Last & Patrick McLeavey
Recipes Christine France, Roz Denny, Catherine Atkinson, Liz Trigg,
Rosamund Grant, Sarah Gates, Carole Clements, Elizabeth Wolf-Cohen,
Nicola Diggins, Patricia Lousada, Frances Cleary, Sallie Morris, Shirley Gill
& Norma MacMillan

For all recipes, quantities are given in both metric and imperial measures, and, where
appropriate, measures are also given in standard cups and spoons. Follow one set, but not
a mixture, because they are not interchangeable.

Printed in China

Contents

Introduction

It is no wonder people talk about the spice of life — these aromatic flavourings lift the everyday into the realms of romance. Once so precious and rare that wars were fought over them and men travelled thousands of miles in their pursuit, spices are now no further away than the nearest supermarket.

They remain mysterious, however, despite the rise in the popularity of Indian, Thai, Vietnamese and Chinese dishes, and many people prefer to plump for a prepared spice mixture than to experiment with roasting, grinding and blending their own spices. This is a pity, for becoming familiar with spices is a rewarding experience. Learning which types are pungent and which are mild, and discovering which are your particular favourites, means that you can make up mixtures to suit your own tastes, and the tastes of your family and friends. It's a common misconception that all spices used in curries are hot and fiery, yet nothing could be further from the truth. Spicy dishes can be subtle, pungent, aromatic, fragrant — the choice is in your own hands when you are the one wielding the pestle or operating the grinder.

Even chillies, which many nervous cooks distrust, can add piquancy rather than punch, if only the flesh is used and that in small quantities. As for root ginger, reach out for those knobbly hands — until you've grated fresh ginger into a stir-fry you've missed out on a great culinary treat.

Make more of spices: flavour your sugar with a vanilla pod; greet winter guests with wine mulled with nutmeg and cinnamon; stud oranges closely with cloves for a scented centrepiece for a beautiful Christmas table. Try five spice powder, that interesting combination of star anise, Szechuan peppercorns, fennel, cloves and cinnamon, so highly favoured by Chinese cooks; make more use of aromatic seeds like dill seed, juniper berries, aniseed and coriander seeds.

What's the difference between herbs and spices? This is quite a confusing issue, as one plant can appear to produce both. Generally speaking, herbs are the leaves of culinary plants, usually native to temperate regions of the globe, whereas spices come from tropical or subtropical plants (often shrubs or trees), and may be bark, berries, buds, flower stigmas, fruit or roots. Spices are generally dried before use. The

seeds of culinary plants are frequently also categorised as spices, so the leafy coriander is a herb, but coriander seeds — which, incidentally, have a very different flavour — are regarded as spices.

Both herbs and spices have long been valued for their medicinal qualities. Aniseed aids digestion, as does dill seed, which explains why the latter is often cooked with cabbage. Nutmeg is said to stimulate the appetite, and juniper berries to ease arthritis pain. Cinnamon has been credited with being an aphrodisiac, which might explain that optimistic custom of stirring bedtime black coffee with a cinnamon stick! When used wisely, alone or in combination, spices can transform your cooking and can truly be a cook's best friend.

7

Familiar Spices

ANISE

The oval, grey-green seeds (aniseed) of this aromatic annual plant have a sweet liquorice-like flavour and are used in baking and to flavour liqueurs.

CARDAMOM

Tiny black seeds encased in pale green or parchment-coloured pods, cardamom is valued for its pungent flavour and used in curries, soups and some milk puddings. The pods may be bruised and used whole, or the seeds used on their own.

CAYENNE

Cayenne and paprika are ground spices, made from various peppers. Cayenne is very hot; paprika is often mild but can be fiery. Chilli powder comes from ground dried red chillies and is usually hot.

CARAWAY SEEDS

Harvested from a leafy biennial plant, the seeds are used in cakes, breads, some pork dishes and with potatoes and cabbage. ·

CINNAMON

The bark of a tropical evergreen tree, which is sold either as quills (sticks) or ground, cinnamon has a sweet, pungent flavour. It is widely used, especially in puddings and cakes, with stewed fruit and mulled wine.

ALLSPICE

The sun-dried fruit of a tropical evergreen tree, allspice berries are used in baking, pickling and to flavour stews and sauces. The flavour resembles a blend of cinnamon, cloves and nutmeg.

CLOVES

Resembling small black nails, these are the dried, unopened flower pods of a tropical tree. Whole or ground cloves are used in baking, pickling and hot punches.

CORIANDER

The dried beige-coloured seeds of this member of the parsley family have a light spicy taste, strengthened by roasting. Use whole or ground, in curries and casseroles.

SAFFRON

The world's most precious spice, saffron consists of the dried stigmas of a type of crocus. Valued for both the flavour and the deep yellow colour it gives to food, saffron should be bought from a reputable source. Use threads in preference to powder.

NUTMEG

Like mace, nutmeg comes from a tropical tree. Nutmeg is the seed kernel and mace its fibrous outer case. Both are available ground, but for the best sweet, warm flavour, use blades of mace or grate your own nutmeg as required.

TURMERIC

Like saffron, this powdered root of a member of the ginger family tints food yellow, but the flavour does not compare. Turmeric has a strong woody taste and is best used in curries and pickles.

SESAME SEEDS

Popular in breads and biscuits, and as a source of a flavoursome oil, these small oval seeds come from a tropical annual plant. They should be roasted before use.

CUMIN

Often confused with caraway, which it resembles in appearance and taste, cumin seeds come from a leafy plant related to parsley. The whole or ground spice is often used in Indian and Mexican cooking.

GINGER

A knobbly rhizome of a tropical plant, this is a popular ingredient in many sweet and savoury dishes, and is used fresh (grated or chopped), crystallized, preserved in syrup or ground. Use fresh where possible.

Techniques

GRATING NUTMEG

Multi-purpose box graters usually have a very fine section for nutmeg. Miniature graters, designed for this spice, are also available. Grate fresh nutmeg on milk puddings, over layered potatoes ready for baking with cream, and into cake and biscuit mixes.

GRINDING SPICES

Dry roast selected spices (for recipes see opposite) in a heavy-based frying pan. When cool, tip in to a mortar and grind with a pestle. Alternatively – and this is well worth doing if you enjoy spicy foods – invest in a coffee grinder to be used solely for spices and spice mixes, such as Garam Masala or your own blend of curry powder.

USING FRESH GINGER

Fresh root ginger will keep in the fridge for up to 3 weeks, either in a polythene bag or peeled and placed in a glass jar with sherry to cover (after use, save the liquor for sauces and dressings). Root ginger can also be frozen, then grated or shaved directly into stir-fries and sauces.

USING SAFFRON

Because saffron is so expensive, it is widely imitated. It is best to buy the whole dried stigmas (threads) from a reputable supplier. Grind the threads in a mortar with a pestle (or use the end of a rolling pin in a sturdy bowl), then dissolve the powder in hot water or stock before use.

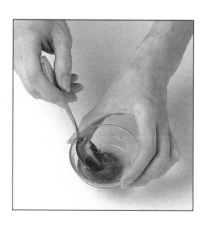

Spice Mixes

GARAM MASALA

This popular spice blend is widely used in Indian cooking, and is usually added towards the end of the cooking time. Place a heavy-based frying pan over a moderate heat. Add the seeds from 4 green cardamom pods with 30ml/2 tbsp each of cumin and coriander seeds, 10ml/2 tsp each of whole cloves and black peppercorns and a crumbled cinnamon stick. Cook, stirring, until roasted. Cool, then grind in a mortar with a pestle. Grate in half a nutmeg before using.

CURRY POWDER

Experiment to find the spice blend you like best. For starters, try mixing 15ml/1 tbsp each of dry-roasted cumin seeds, fenugreek seeds and black peppercorns. Add 60ml/4 tbsp dry-roasted coriander seeds and 5ml/1 tsp mustard seeds. Grind to a fine powder, then stir in 15ml/1 tbsp ground turmeric, 10ml/2 tsp ground ginger and 5ml/1 tsp mild chilli powder.

FIVE SPICE POWDER

Crumble 2 cinnamon sticks into a mortar. Add 10ml/2 tsp each crumbled star anise, anise pepper (ground Szechuan peppercorns), fennel seeds and whole cloves. Grind to a powder and use sparingly.

11

COOK'S TIP

Keep home-made spice mixes in airtight containers in a cool, dry place out of direct sunlight. They are best used as soon as possible — if you must store spice mixes for more than a month, keep them in tightly covered tubs in the freezer.

Starters &
Snacks

Spiced Parsnip Soup

INGREDIENTS

40g / 1½oz / 3 tbsp butter
1 onion, chopped
675g / 1½lb parsnips, diced
5ml / 1 tsp ground coriander
2.5ml / ½ tsp ground cumin
2.5ml / ½ tsp ground turmeric
1.25ml / ¼ tsp chilli powder
1.2 litres / 2 pints / 5 cups chicken stock
150ml / ¼ pint / ⅔ cup single cream
15ml / 1 tbsp sunflower oil
1 garlic clove, cut in julienne strips
10ml / 2 tsp yellow mustard seeds
salt and ground black pepper

SERVES 4–6

1 Melt the butter in a large pan, add the onion and parsnips and fry gently for about 3 minutes.

2 Stir in the spices. Cook for about 1 minute, add the stock, season, and bring to the boil. Cover, then simmer for 45 minutes, or until the parsnips are tender.

3 Cool slightly, then purée in a blender until smooth. Return the soup to the pan, add the cream and heat through gently over a low heat.

4 Heat the oil in a small pan, add the julienne strips of garlic and yellow mustard seeds and fry quickly until the garlic is beginning to brown and the mustard seeds start to pop and splutter. Remove the pan from the heat.

5 Ladle the soup into warmed soup bowls and pour a little of the hot spice mixture over each. Serve at once.

13

Spicy Vegetable Fritters with Thai Salsa

INGREDIENTS

10ml/2 tsp cumin seeds
10ml/2 tsp coriander seeds
115g/4oz/1 cup chick-pea (gram) flour
2.5ml/½ tsp bicarbonate of soda
120ml/4fl oz/½ cup warm water
120ml/4fl oz/½ cup groundnut oil
450g/1lb courgettes, cut in 7.5cm/3in sticks
salt and ground black pepper
fresh mint sprigs, to garnish
THAI SALSA
½ cucumber, diced
3 spring onions, chopped
6 radishes, cubed
30ml/2 tbsp chopped fresh mint
2.5cm/1in piece of root ginger, peeled and grated
45ml/3 tbsp lime juice
30ml/2 tbsp caster sugar
3 garlic cloves, crushed

SERVES 2–4

1 Heat the wok. Add the cumin and coriander seeds. Toast them, turning them over frequently. Cool them, then grind well, using a pestle and mortar.

2 Blend the flour, bicarbonate of soda, spices and salt and pepper in a food processor. Add the warm water and 15ml/1 tbsp of the oil, and blend again. Tip into a bowl.

3 Coat the courgettes in the batter, then leave to stand for 10 minutes. Meanwhile make the Thai salsa by mixing all the ingredients together in a bowl.

4 Heat the wok, then add the remaining oil. When the oil is hot, stir-fry the courgettes in batches. Drain well on kitchen paper, then serve hot with the salsa, garnished with fresh mint sprigs.

COOK'S TIP
The Thai salsa goes just as well with plain stir-fried salmon strips or stir-fried beef as it does with these courgette fritters.

14

Mixed Spiced Nuts

INGREDIENTS

*75g/ 3oz/ 1 cup dried unsweetened
coconut flakes
75ml/ 5 tbsp peanut oil
2.5ml/ ½ tsp chilli powder
5ml/ 1 tsp ground paprika
5ml/ 1 tsp tomato purée
225g/ 8oz/ 2 cups unsalted cashew nuts
225g/ 8oz/ 2 cups whole blanched almonds
60ml/ 4 tbsp caster sugar
5ml/ 1 tsp ground cumin
2.5ml/ ½ tsp salt
ground black pepper
paprika, mustard and cress, to garnish*

SERVES 4–6

16

1 Heat the wok, add the dried coconut flakes and dry-fry until golden. Leave to cool.

2 Heat the wok and add 45ml/3 tbsp of the peanut oil. When the oil is hot, add the chilli, paprika and tomato purée. Gently stir-fry the cashews in the spicy mix until well coated. Drain well and season. Leave to cool.

3 Wipe out the wok with kitchen paper, heat it, then add the remaining oil. When the oil is hot, add the blanched almonds and sprinkle in the sugar. Stir-fry gently until the almonds are golden and the sugar is caramelized. Place the cumin and salt in a bowl. Add the almonds, toss well, then leave to cool.

4 Mix the cashews, almonds and coconut flakes together or serve in separate bowls. Sprinkle with paprika and garnish with mustard and cress.

Spicy Meat Patties with Coconut

INGREDIENTS

*115g/4oz/1⅓ cups freshly grated coconut, or
desiccated coconut soaked in 60-90ml/
4-6 tbsp boiling water
350g/12oz/1½ cups finely minced beef
2.5ml/½ tsp each coriander and cumin seeds,
dry-fried
1 garlic clove, crushed
a little beaten egg
15-30ml/1-2 tbsp plain flour
groundnut oil, for frying
salt
thin lemon and lime wedges, to serve*

MAKES 22

1 Mix the fresh or soaked desiccated coconut with the minced beef. (It is not necessary to add water to fresh coconut.)

3 Divide the meat into evenly-sized portions, the size of a walnut, and form into patty shapes. Dust lightly with flour.

2 Grind the dry-fried coriander and cumin seeds in a pestle and mortar. Add to the meat mixture with the garlic, salt to taste, and enough beaten egg to bind.

4 Heat the oil and then fry the patties for 4–5 minutes until both sides are golden brown and cooked through. Serve with lemon and lime wedges, to squeeze over.

Plantain Crisps

INGREDIENTS

vegetable oil, for shallow frying
2 green plantains
½ onion
1 yellow plantain
pinch of garlic granules
cayenne pepper
salt

SERVES 4

18

2 Fry the plantain rounds in the oil for about 3 minutes, turning until golden brown. Drain on kitchen paper and keep hot.

3 Coarsely grate the other green plantain and put on a plate. Slice the onion into wafer-thin shreds with a sharp knife and mix with the grated plantain.

4 Heat a little more oil in the frying pan and fry handfuls of the onion mixture for 2–3 minutes, until golden, turning once. Drain and keep hot.

5 Heat a little more oil in the frying pan and, while it is heating, peel the yellow plantain, cut in half lengthways and dice. Sprinkle with the garlic

granules and cayenne. Fry until golden brown, turning to brown evenly. Drain on kitchen paper and then arrange the three varieties of cooked plantains in shallow dishes. Sprinkle with salt and serve.

1 Heat the oil in a large frying pan over a moderate heat. While the oil is heating, peel one of the green plantains and pare thinly into very neat rounds.

Spicy Kebabs

INGREDIENTS

450g/1lb frying steak
2.5ml/½ tsp caster sugar
5ml/1 tsp garlic granules
5ml/1 tsp ground ginger
5ml/1 tsp paprika
5ml/1 tsp ground cinnamon
pinch of chilli powder
10ml/2 tsp onion salt
50g/2oz/½ cup peanuts, finely crushed
vegetable oil, for brushing
red onion rings, to garnish (optional)

SERVES 4

1 Trim the steak of any fat and then cut into 2.5cm/1in wide strips. Place in a bowl or a shallow dish and chill until required.

2 Mix the sugar, garlic granules, spices and onion salt together in a small bowl with the crushed nuts. Mix well, then press the mixture into the steak.

3 Thread all the spicy steak on to eight satay sticks. Push the strips together closely. Place the kebabs in a shallow dish, cover them loosely with foil and leave to marinate in a cool place for a few hours to allow the flavours to develop.

4 Preheat a grill or barbecue. Brush the meat with a little oil and then cook on a moderate heat for about 15 minutes, until evenly browned. Turn the kebabs frequently to cook them evenly. Serve at once, with red onion rings, if you like.

Spiced Honey Chicken Wings

INGREDIENTS

1 red chilli, finely chopped
5ml/1 tsp chilli powder
5ml/1 tsp ground ginger
finely grated rind of 1 lime
12 chicken wings
60ml/4 tbsp sunflower oil
15ml/1 tbsp fresh coriander, chopped
30ml/2 tbsp soy sauce
45ml/3 tbsp clear honey
lime slices, to serve

SERVES 4

1 Mix the fresh chilli, chilli powder, ground ginger and the lime rind together. Rub the mixture into the chicken wings and chill them for at least 2 hours.

2 Heat half the oil in a wok. When it is hot, add half the wings. Fry for 10 minutes, turning often, until crisp and golden. Drain on kitchen paper. Repeat with the remaining oil and chicken wings.

3 Add the coriander to the hot wok and stir-fry for 30 seconds, then return the wings to the wok and stir-fry the mixture for 1 minute more.

4 Stir in the soy sauce and honey, and stir-fry for 1 minute. Serve the spiced honey chicken wings at once, with the lime slices to squeeze over the top.

Fish Dishes

Cajun Spiced Fish

INGREDIENTS

5ml / 1 tsp dried thyme
5 ml / 1 tsp dried oregano
5 ml / 1 tsp ground black pepper
1.5 ml / ¼ tsp cayenne pepper
10 ml / 2 tsp paprika
2.5 ml / ½ tsp garlic salt
4 tail end pieces of cod fillet,
about 175g / 6 oz each
75g / 3oz / 6 tbsp butter
½ red pepper, seeded and sliced
½ green pepper, seeded and sliced
fresh thyme, to garnish
grilled tomatoes and mashed sweet
potato, to serve

SERVES 4

1 Place all the herbs and spices in a bowl and mix well. Dip the fish fillets in the spice mixture until they are lightly coated. Heat 25g/1oz/ 2 tbsp of the butter in a large frying pan, add the peppers and fry for 4–5 minutes, until softened. Remove the peppers with a slotted spoon and keep hot.

2 Add the rest of the butter to the pan and heat until sizzling. Add the fish fillets and fry on a moderate heat for 3–4 minutes on each side, until they are browned.

3 Transfer the fish to a warmed serving dish and surround with the peppers. Garnish with thyme. Serve the spiced fish with some grilled tomatoes and plenty of mashed sweet potato.

Spiced Salmon Stir-fry

INGREDIENTS

4 salmon steaks, about 225g/8oz each
4 whole star anise
1 dried red chilli, seeded (optional)
2 lemon grass stalks, sliced
finely grated rind and juice of 3 limes
30ml/2 tbsp clear honey
30ml/2 tbsp grapeseed oil
salt and ground black pepper
lime wedges, to garnish

SERVES 4

1 Remove the middle bone from each salmon steak using a very sharp filleting knife, to make two neat strips from each piece of fish.

2 Holding the fish firmly, neatly cut off the skin – a little salt on your fingers may help your grip. Cut the fish into pieces, if you like, and place it in a glass bowl.

3 Coarsely crush the star anise in a pestle and mortar with the chilli, if using. Add to the the salmon with the lemon grass, lime rind and juice, and honey, and toss to coat. Season well with salt and pepper, cover and place in the fridge to marinate overnight.

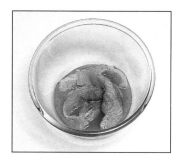

4 Carefully drain the salmon, reserving all the marinade, and pat dry on kitchen paper.

5 Heat a wok, then add the oil. When the oil is hot, add the salmon and stir-fry, stirring constantly until cooked. Increase the heat, pour over the lime marinade and bring to the boil. Serve at once, with a garnish of lime wedges.

COOK'S TIP
Marinating the salmon allows all the flavours to develop, and the lime tenderizes the fish beautifully, so it needs very little stir-frying. Be careful not to overcook it.

24

Louisiana Cod

INGREDIENTS

30ml/2 tbsp natural yogurt
15ml/1 tbsp lemon or lime juice
4 cod steaks, about 175g/6oz each
1 garlic clove, crushed
5ml/1 tsp ground cumin
5ml/1 tsp paprika
5ml/1 tsp mustard powder
2.5ml/½ tsp cayenne pepper
2.5ml/½ tsp dried thyme
2.5ml/½ tsp dried oregano
lemon slices, to garnish
new potatoes and a mixed salad, to serve

SERVES 4

1 Mix the yogurt and lemon or lime juice and brush lightly over the fish. Combine the garlic, spices and herbs and rub into both sides of the fish, coating well.

2 Lightly grease a ridged grill pan or heavy-based frying pan. Heat until very hot. Add the fish and cook over a high heat for 4 minutes, or until the underside of each steak is well browned.

3 Turn the cod steaks over and cook for a further 4 minutes, or until they have cooked through. Garnish with lemon slices and serve at once, with new potatoes and a mixed salad.

COOK'S TIP
This recipe works equally well with any firm-fleshed fish, such as swordfish, shark, tuna or halibut.

Spicy Crab & Coconut

INGREDIENTS

40g/1½oz/½ cup dried unsweetened
coconut flakes
2 garlic cloves
5cm/2in piece of root ginger, peeled and grated
2.5ml/½ tsp cumin seeds
1 small cinnamon stick
2.5ml/½ tsp ground turmeric
2 dried red chillies
15ml/1 tbsp coriander seeds
2.5ml/½ tsp poppy seeds
15ml/1 tbsp vegetable oil
1 onion, sliced
1 small green pepper, seeded and cut in strips
16 crab claws
fresh coriander sprigs,
to garnish
150ml/¼ pint/⅔ cup natural yogurt,
to serve (optional)

SERVES 4

1 Place the dried coconut, garlic, ginger, cumin seeds, cinnamon, turmeric, red chillies, coriander and poppy seeds in a food processor and process until well blended.

2 Heat the oil in a wok and fry the onion until soft, but not coloured. Add the green pepper.

3 Stir in the spice mixture and stir-fry for 1 minute.

4 Remove all of the vegetables with a slotted spoon. Heat the wok. Add the crab claws, stir-fry for 2 minutes, then briefly return all the spiced vegetables to the wok and heat through. Garnish with fresh coriander sprigs and serve with natural yogurt, if you like.

Fish Curry

INGREDIENTS

675g / 1½lb white boneless fish such as halibut,
cod, coley or monkfish
juice of ½ lime
5ml / 1 tsp cider vinegar
225g / 8oz / 2⅔ cups grated fresh coconut
2.5cm / 1in piece of root ginger, peeled
and grated
6 garlic cloves
450g / 1lb tomatoes, chopped
45ml / 3 tbsp sunflower oil
350g / 12oz onions, roughly chopped
20 curry leaves
5ml / 1 tsp ground coriander
2.5ml / ½ tsp ground turmeric
10ml / 2 tsp ground chilli
300ml / ½ pint / 1¼ cups water
2.5ml / ½ tsp fenugreek seeds
2.5ml / ½ tsp cumin seeds
salt and ground black pepper
lime slices and fresh coconut slivers, to garnish

SERVES 4

1 Marinate the fish, in a shallow bowl, in the lime juice, vinegar and a pinch of salt, for 30 minutes.

2 In a food processor fitted with a metal blade, process the grated coconut, ginger, garlic cloves and tomatoes to make a paste.

3 Heat the oil in a frying pan, add the onions and cook until golden brown, then add the curry leaves.

4 Add the ground coriander, turmeric and chilli and stir-fry for 1 minute.

5 Add the coconut paste and cook for 3–4 minutes, stirring constantly. Pour in the water, bring to the boil, lower the heat and simmer for 4 minutes.

6 In the meantime pound the fenugreek and cumin seeds together in a pestle and mortar. Lay the fish on top of the sauce in the frying pan, sprinkle it evenly  with the fenugreek mixture and cook for about 15 minutes or until the fish is tender. Lift out the fish, chop it into bite-size pieces and return these to the sauce. Heat through briefly, then serve, garnished with the lime slices and fresh coconut.

Lobster Piri Piri

INGREDIENTS

2 cooked lobsters, halved
fresh coriander sprigs, to garnish
white rice, to serve
PIRI PIRI SAUCE
60ml/4 tbsp vegetable oil
2 onions, chopped
5ml/1 tsp chopped fresh root ginger
450g/1lb fresh or canned tomatoes, chopped
15ml/1 tbsp tomato purée
225g/8oz peeled cooked prawns
10ml/2 tsp ground coriander
1 green chilli, seeded and chopped
15ml/1 tbsp ground dried shrimps or crayfish
1 green pepper, seeded and sliced
600ml/1 pint/2½ cups water
salt and ground black pepper

SERVES 2–4

1 Make the sauce. Heat the oil in a large saucepan, add the onions, ginger, tomatoes and purée, and fry gently for 5 minutes, or until the onions are tender.

2 Add the prawns, ground coriander, chilli and ground shrimps or crayfish and stir well to mix.

3 Stir in the green pepper, water and salt and pepper. Bring to the boil and then simmer, uncovered, over a moderate heat for 20–30 minutes until thickened.

4 Pour the sauce into a flameproof casserole and add the lobsters. Heat through. Arrange the lobster halves on a bed of rice on 2–4 warmed serving plates and pour the sauce over each portion. Garnish with a few coriander sprigs and serve piping hot.

30

Meat Dishes

Moroccan Spiced Roast Poussins

INGREDIENTS

115g/4oz/1 cup cooked long-grain rice
1 small onion, finely chopped
finely grated rind and juice of 1 lemon
30ml/2 tbsp chopped mint
45ml/3 tbsp chopped dried apricots
30ml/2 tbsp natural yogurt
10ml/2 tsp ground turmeric
10ml/2 tsp ground cumin
2 x 450g/1lb poussins
salt and ground black pepper
lemon slices and mint sprigs, to garnish
mixed rice and wild rice, to serve

SERVES 4

1 Preheat the oven to 200°C/400°F/Gas 6. Mix together the rice, onion, lemon rind, mint and apricots. Stir in half each of the lemon juice, yogurt, turmeric, cumin, and add salt and pepper.

2 Stuff both the poussins with the rice mixture at the neck end only. Any spare stuffing can be cooked in a dish. Place the poussins on a rack in a roasting tin.

3 Mix together the remaining lemon juice, yogurt, turmeric and cumin, then brush this over the poussins. Cover the birds loosely with foil and cook in the oven for 30 minutes.

4 Remove the foil and roast for 15 minutes more until the birds are golden brown and the juices run clear, not pink, when the thighs are pierced. Cut the poussins in half with a sharp knife or poultry shears, and serve with the extra stuffing or a mixture of rice and wild rice. Garnish with lemon slices and fresh mint sprigs.

Roast Wild Duck with Juniper

INGREDIENTS

15ml / 1 tbsp juniper berries, fresh if possible
1 oven-ready wild duck (preferably a mallard)
25g / 1oz / 2 tbsp butter, softened
45ml / 3 tbsp gin
120ml / 4fl oz / ½ cup duck or chicken stock
120ml / 4fl oz / ½ cup whipping cream
salt and ground black pepper
watercress, to garnish

SERVES 2

1 Preheat the oven to 230°C/450°F/Gas 8. Reserve a few juniper berries for garnishing and put the remainder in a heavy polythene bag. Crush the berries coarsely with a rolling pin.

2 Wipe the duck with damp kitchen paper and remove any excess fat or skin. Spread with butter and season well, then pat all over with the crushed berries.

3 Place the duck in a roasting tin and roast for 20–25 minutes, basting occasionally; the juices should run slightly pink when the thigh is pierced with a knife. Pour the juices from the cavity into the roasting tin and transfer the duck to a carving board. Cover with foil; leave for 10–15 minutes.

4 Meanwhile, skim off most of the fat from the roasting tin, leaving as many of the juniper berries as possible, and place the tin over a medium-high heat. Add the gin. Stir, scraping the base of the tin. Bring to the boil. Cook until the liquid has almost evaporated, then add the stock and boil to reduce by half. Add the cream and boil for 2 minutes more, or until the sauce thickens slightly. Strain into a small saucepan and keep warm.

5 Carve the legs from the duck and separate the thigh from the drumstick. Remove the breasts and arrange the duck in a warmed serving dish. Pour a little sauce over, sprinkle with the reserved juniper berries and garnish with watercress.

COOK'S TIP
If you do not serve the legs, use the legs and duck carcass to make a duck stock for use in other game dishes.

34

Chicken in Spicy Yogurt

INGREDIENTS

6 chicken pieces
juice of 1 lemon
5ml / 1 tsp salt
MARINADE
5ml / 1 tsp coriander seeds
10ml / 2 tsp cumin seeds
6 cloves
2 bay leaves
1 onion, quartered
2 garlic cloves
5cm / 2in piece of root ginger, peeled
and roughly chopped
2.5ml / ½ tsp chilli powder
5ml / 1 tsp turmeric
150ml / ¼ pint / ⅔ cup natural yogurt
lemon wedges and mint sprigs, to garnish
mixed salad leaves, to serve

SERVES 6

1 Skin the chicken pieces and make deep slashes in the fleshiest parts with a sharp knife. Place in a shallow dish, sprinkle over the lemon and salt, and rub in well.

2 Make the marinade. Spread the coriander and cumin seeds, cloves and bay leaves in a large frying pan and dry-fry until the bay leaves are crisp.

3 Cool the spices and grind them coarsely in a mortar with a pestle.

4 Finely chop the onion, garlic and ginger in a food processor or blender. Add the ground spices, chilli powder, turmeric and yogurt, then strain in the lemon juice from the chicken.

5 Arrange all the chicken in a single layer in a roasting tin. Pour over the marinade, then cover and chill for 24–36 hours, regularly turning the chicken pieces.

6 Preheat the oven to 200°C/400°F/Gas 6. Cook the chicken for 45 minutes. Serve hot or cold, garnished with slices of lemon and fresh mint, accompanied with a few mixed salad leaves.

VARIATION
This marinade will also work well brushed over skewers of lamb or pork fillet.

36

Pork Roasted with Herbs, Spices & Rum

INGREDIENTS

2 garlic cloves, crushed
45ml/3 tbsp soy sauce
15ml/1 tbsp malt vinegar
15ml/1 tbsp finely chopped celery
30ml/2 tbsp chopped spring onion
7.5ml/1½ tsp dried thyme
5ml/1 tsp dried sage
2.5ml/½ tsp mixed spice
15ml/1 tbsp demerara sugar
10ml/2 tsp curry powder
120ml/4fl oz/½ cup rum
1.5kg/3-3½lb joint of pork, boned and scored
salt and ground black pepper
spring onion curls, to garnish
SAUCE
25g/1oz/2 tbsp butter or margarine
15ml/1 tbsp tomato purée
300ml/½ pint/1¼ cups stock
15ml/1 tbsp chopped fresh parsley
15ml/1 tbsp demerara sugar
Tabasco sauce, to taste
salt

SERVES 6–8

1 Mix together the garlic, soy sauce, vinegar, celery, spring onion, thyme, sage, mixed spice, demerara sugar, curry powder, rum, and salt and pepper.

2 Open out the pork. Slash the meat but do not cut it through. Spread the spice mixture all over the meat and press it in well. Chill overnight.

3 Preheat the oven to 190°C/375°F/Gas 5. Roll the meat up, then tie tightly in several places with strong cotton string to hold it in place. Spread a large piece of foil across a roasting tin and place the pork in the centre. Baste the pork with a few spoonfuls of the marinade and wrap the foil around it, holding in the marinade.

4 Bake in the oven for 1¾ hours, then remove the foil, baste with any remaining marinade and cook for 1 hour more. Check occasionally that the pork is not drying out and baste with any pan juices.

5 Transfer the pork to a warmed serving dish and leave to stand in a warm place for 15 minutes before serving. Meanwhile, make the sauce. Pour the pan juices into a small saucepan, add the butter or margarine, the tomato purée, stock, parsley, sugar, Tabasco and salt to taste. Simmer gently until reduced. Serve the pork sliced, garnished with spring onion curls. Serve the sauce separately.

38

Steak au Poivre

INGREDIENTS

30ml/2 tbsp black peppercorns
2 fillet or sirloin steaks, about 225g/8oz each
15g/½oz/1 tbsp butter
10ml/2 tsp vegetable oil
45ml/3 tbsp brandy
150ml/¼ pint/⅔ cup whipping cream
1 garlic clove, finely chopped
salt, if needed

SERVES 2

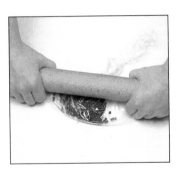

I Place the black peppercorns in a plastic bag. Crush with a rolling pin or the flat base of a heavy pan until medium-coarse, or crush in a mortar with a pestle.

2 Put the steaks on a board. Press the pepper on to both sides of the meat, coating it completely.

3 Melt the butter with the oil in a heavy frying pan over a medium-high heat. Add the meat and cook, turning once, until done as preferred (rare meat will still  be fairly soft when pressed, medium-rare will be slightly soft, medium will be springy and well-done firm). Transfer the steaks to a warmed platter or plates and cover with foil to keep them hot.

4 Pour in the brandy to deglaze the pan. Allow to boil until reduced by half, scraping the base of the pan, then add the cream and garlic. Boil gently over a  medium heat for about 4 minutes, until the cream has reduced by one-third. Stir any accumulated juices from the meat into the sauce, taste and add salt, if necessary. Serve the steaks with the brandy and cream sauce.

Moroccan Lamb Stew

INGREDIENTS

60ml/4 tbsp olive oil
10ml/2 tsp caster sugar
10ml/2 tsp ground cumin
5ml/1 tsp ground cinnamon
5ml/1 tsp ground ginger
2.5ml/½ tsp ground turmeric
2.5ml/½ tsp powdered saffron or paprika
*1.3kg/3lb lamb shoulder, trimmed of all fat
and cut in 5cm/2in pieces*
2 onions, coarsely chopped
3 garlic cloves, finely chopped
250ml/8fl oz/1 cup lamb stock
2 tomatoes, peeled, seeded and chopped
425g/15oz can chick-peas, drained
*75g/3oz/⅔ cup raisins, soaked in warm
water for 10 minutes*
10-24 stoned black olives (such as Kalamata)
*2 preserved lemons, thinly sliced, or grated
rind of 1 unwaxed lemon*
60-90ml/4-6 tbsp chopped fresh coriander
salt and ground black pepper
couscous, to serve

SERVES 6–8

1 In a large bowl, combine half the olive oil with the sugar, cumin, cinnamon, ginger, turmeric, saffron or paprika, pepper and 5ml/1 tsp salt.

2 Add the lamb to the spice mixture, toss to coat well and set aside for at least 20 minutes to allow the flavours to develop.

3 Heat the remaining oil in a large heavy frying pan. Brown the lamb pieces evenly, in batches, then transfer to a large flameproof casserole.

4 Add the onions to the frying pan and stir them until well browned. Stir in the garlic, stock and chopped tomatoes. Tip into the casserole, add water to cover and bring to the boil over a high heat, skimming off any foam that rises to the surface. Reduce the heat to low and simmer for about 1 hour, or until the meat is tender.

5 Add the chick-peas to the lamb in the casserole with about 250ml/8fl oz/1 cup water. Stir in the raisins and their soaking liquid and simmer for 30 minutes  more. Stir in the olives and sliced preserved lemons or lemon rind and simmer for 20–30 minutes more. Stir in half the chopped fresh coriander. To serve, spoon the couscous on to a warmed serving dish, spoon the lamb stew on top and sprinkle with the remaining fresh coriander.

Desserts

Spiced Nutty Bananas

INGREDIENTS

6 ripe but firm bananas
30ml/2 tbsp chopped unsalted cashew nuts
30ml/2 tbsp chopped unsalted peanuts
30ml/2 tbsp desiccated coconut
7.5-15ml/½-1 tbsp demerara sugar
5ml/1 tsp ground cinnamon, plus extra
for dusting
2.5ml/½ tsp freshly grated nutmeg
60ml/4 tbsp rum
150ml/¼ pint/⅔ cup orange juice
15g/½oz/1 tbsp butter
crème fraîche or double cream, to serve

SERVES 3

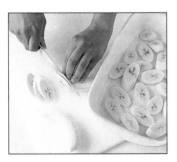

1 Preheat the oven to 200°C/400°F/ Gas 6. Slice the bananas and place them in a greased, shallow ovenproof dish. Mix the cashews, peanuts, coconut, sugar, cinnamon and nutmeg in a bowl. Pour the rum and juice over the bananas; sprinkle with the nut mix.

2 Dot the top with butter, then bake in the oven for 15–20 minutes or until the bananas are golden and the sauce is bubbly. Serve at once with crème fraîche or double cream, dusted with cinnamon.

COOK'S TIP
Freshly grated nutmeg makes all the difference to this dish. More rum can be added if you like. Chopped mixed nuts can be used instead of cashew nuts and peanuts.

Cinnamon & Apricot Soufflés

INGREDIENTS

3 eggs
115g/4oz/½ cup apricot fruit spread
finely grated rind of ½ lemon
5ml/1 tsp ground cinnamon, plus extra
to decorate
flour, for dusting

SERVES 4

1 Preheat the oven to 190°C/375°F/Gas 5. Lightly grease four individual soufflé dishes and dust them lightly with flour.

2 Separate the eggs and place the yolks in a bowl with the fruit spread, lemon rind and cinnamon. Whisk hard until the mixture is thick and pale.

3 Place the egg whites in a clean bowl and whisk them until they are stiff enough to hold soft peaks.

4 Using a metal spoon or spatula, fold the egg whites evenly into the yolk mixture, taking care to knock out as little air as possible.

5 Divide the spicy soufflé mixture between the prepared dishes and bake for about 10–15 minutes, or until well-risen and pale gold on the top. Place each soufflé dish on an individual plate and serve at once, dusted with a little extra ground cinnamon.

COOK'S TIP

Puréed fresh or well drained canned apricots can be used instead of the apricot spread, but make sure the mixture is not too wet, or the soufflé will not rise properly. Also, try using other fruits, such as fresh or canned pears or peaches.

Ginger Baked Pears

INGREDIENTS

4 large pears
300ml / ½ pint / 1¼ cups whipping cream
50g / 2oz / ¼ cup caster sugar
2.5ml / ½ tsp vanilla essence
1.5ml / ¼ tsp ground cinnamon
pinch of freshly grated nutmeg
5ml / 1 tsp grated fresh root ginger

SERVES 4

1 Preheat the oven to 190°C/375°F/Gas 5. Lightly butter a large shallow baking dish.

2 Peel the pears, cut in half lengthways and remove the cores. Arrange, cut-side down, in a single layer in the baking dish. Mix the cream with the caster sugar and  vanilla essence. Add the cinnamon, nutmeg and ginger and pour the mixture over the pears.

3 Bake for 30–35 minutes, basting from time to time, until the pears are tender and browned on top and the cream is thick and bubbly. Set aside to cool slightly before serving.

COOK'S TIP
Try to find Comice or Anjou pears - the recipe is useful for slightly under-ripe fruit.

Spiced Peach Crumble

INGREDIENTS

1.3kg / 3lb ripe but firm peaches, peeled, stoned
and sliced
60ml / 4 tbsp caster sugar
2.5ml / ½ tsp ground cinnamon
5ml / 1 tsp lemon juice
Greek-style yogurt or whipped cream,
to serve (optional)

TOPPING

115g / 4oz / 1 cup plain flour
1.5ml / ¼ tsp ground cinnamon
1.5ml / ¼ tsp ground allspice
75g / 3oz / 1 cup rolled oats
175g / 6oz / 1 cup soft light brown sugar
115g / 4oz / ½ cup butter

SERVES 6

1 Preheat the oven to 190°C/375°F/Gas 5. Grease a 20–23cm/8–9 in diameter baking dish.

2 Make the topping. Sift the flour and spices into a bowl. Add the oats and sugar and stir to combine. Cut or rub in the butter until the mixture resembles coarse crumbs.

3 Toss the peaches with the sugar, cinnamon and lemon juice. Put the fruit in the baking dish.

4 Scatter the topping over the fruit in an even layer. Bake for 30–35 minutes and serve warm, with a bowl of creamy Greek yogurt or whipped cream on the side.

VARIATION

Use apricots or nectarines instead of peaches.

Clementines in Cinnamon Caramel

INGREDIENTS

8–12 clementines
225g/8oz/1 cup granulated sugar
300ml/½ pint/1¼ cups boiling water
2 cinnamon sticks
30ml/2 tbsp orange-flavoured liqueur
25g/1oz/¼ cup shelled pistachio nuts
Greek-style yogurt or crème fraîche,
to serve (optional)

SERVES 4–6

2 Gently heat the sugar in a pan until it dissolves and turns a rich golden brown. Immediately turn off the heat to prevent the caramel from darkening.

3 Covering your hand with a dish towel, add 300ml/ ½ pint/1¼ cups of boiling water (the mixture will bubble and may spit). Bring slowly to the boil, stirring until the caramel has dissolved. Add the cinnamon sticks and the strips of peel, then simmer for 5 minutes. Stir in the orange-flavoured liqueur.

4 Cool the syrup for 10 minutes, then pour over the clementines. Cover and chill overnight.

1 Pare the rind from two clementines using a vegetable peeler, taking care to remove none of the white pith. Cut the rind into fine strips and set aside. Cut away the peel from all the clementines, as cleanly as you can, and put them in a bowl.

5 Blanch the nuts in boiling water for a few seconds. Drain, cool and remove the dark outer skin from each nut. Chop the pistachios and scatter over the clementines; serve the dish at once, either on its own or with yogurt or crème fraîche.

Pineapple Wedges with Allspice & Lime

INGREDIENTS

1 medium-size, ripe pineapple
1 lime
15ml / 1 tbsp dark muscovado sugar
5ml / 1 tsp ground allspice

SERVES 4

1 Cut the pineapple lengthways into quarters and remove the core from each piece.

2 Loosen the flesh by sliding a knife between the flesh and the skin. Cut the flesh into slices, leaving it on the skin. Push alternate slices left and right, as illustrated in the main picture.

3 Remove a few shreds of rind from the lime. Cut the fruit in half and squeeze out all of the juice. Sprinkle all of the pineapple pieces with the sugar, fresh lime juice, allspice and rind shreds. Serve at once, or cover the fruit and chill for at least 1 hour.

VARIATION

For a quick hot dish, place the pineapple slices on a baking sheet, sprinkle them with the lime juice, sugar and allspice and place them under a hot grill for 3-4 minutes, or until golden. Sprinkle with the shreds of lime zest and serve.

Spiced Red Fruit Compôte

INGREDIENTS

4 ripe red plums, quartered
225g/8oz/2 cups strawberries, halved
225g/8oz/2 cups raspberries
30ml/2 tbsp light muscovado sugar
30ml/2 tbsp cold water
1 cinnamon stick
3 pieces of star anise
6 cloves
natural yogurt or fromage frais, to serve

SERVES 4

1 Place the plums, strawberries and raspberries in a heavy-based saucepan with the sugar and water.

2 Add the cinnamon stick, star anise and cloves to the pan and heat gently, without boiling, until the sugar dissolves and the juices run from the fruit.

3 Cover the pan and leave the fruit to infuse over a very low heat for about 5 minutes. Remove the spices from the compôte before serving warm with natural yogurt or fromage frais.

Cakes & Bakes

Spiced Date & Walnut Cake

INGREDIENTS

300g / 11oz / 2¾ cups wholemeal
self-raising flour
10ml / 2 tsp mixed spice
150g / 5oz / scant 1 cup chopped dates
50g / 2oz / ½ cup chopped walnuts
60ml / 4 tbsp sunflower oil
115g / 4oz / ½ cup dark muscovado sugar
300ml / ½ pint / 1¼ cups milk
walnut halves, to decorate

SERVES 10–12

1 Preheat the oven to 180°C/350°F/Gas 4. Grease and line a 900g/2lb loaf tin with grease-proof paper or non-stick baking paper.

2 Sift together the flour and spice, adding back any bran from the sieve. Stir in the dates and walnuts.

3 Mix the oil, sugar and milk, then stir evenly into the dry ingredients. Spoon into the prepared tin and arrange the walnut halves on top of the mixture.

4 Bake the cake in the oven for 45–50 minutes, or until golden brown and firm. Turn out the cake, remove the lining paper and leave to cool on a wire rack. Leave for 2 days before cutting.

VARIATION
For a delicious alternative, try using pecan nuts in place of the walnuts in this cake.

55

Apple & Cinnamon Crumble Cake

INGREDIENTS

3 large cooking apples
2.5ml/½ tsp ground cinnamon
225g/8oz/1 cup butter
250g/9oz/scant 1¼ cups caster sugar
4 eggs
450g/1lb/4 cups self-raising flour
CRUMBLE TOPPING
175g/6oz/¾ cup demerara sugar
150g/5oz/1¼ cups plain flour
5ml/1 tsp ground cinnamon
50g/2oz/⅔ cup desiccated coconut
115g/4oz/½ cup butter

SERVES 10–12

2 Peel and core the cooking apples, then grate them coarsely. Place them in a bowl, sprinkle with the cinnamon, toss to coat and set aside.

3 Cream the butter and sugar in a bowl with an electric mixer (or use a food processor), until light and fluffy. Beat in the eggs, one at a time, beating well after each addition. Sift in half the flour, mix well, then add the remaining flour and stir until the mixture is smooth.

4 Spread half the cake mixture evenly over the base of the prepared tin. Spoon the apples on top and scatter over half the crumble topping. Spread the remaining cake mixture over the crumble then top with the remaining crumble topping.

5 Bake for 1 hour 10 minutes–1 hour 20 minutes, covering the cake with foil if it browns too quickly. Leave in the tin for about 5 minutes, before turning out and transferring to a wire rack to cool.

1 Preheat the oven to 180°C/ 350°F/ Gas 4. Grease a 25cm/ 10in round cake tin or a shallow 20cm/8in square tin and line the base with grease-proof paper. Make the crumble topping. Mix together the sugar, flour, cinnamon and coconut in a bowl, rub in the butter with your fingertips until the mixture resembles coarse crumbs, and set aside.

COOK'S TIP
To make the topping in a food processor, add all the ingredients and process for a few seconds until the mixture resembles coarse breadcrumbs.

Ginger Biscuits

INGREDIENTS

250g / 9oz / 2¼ cups plain flour
10ml / 2 tsp ground ginger
2.5ml / ½ tsp grated nutmeg
5ml / 1 tsp ground cinnamon
10ml / 2 tsp baking powder
2.5ml / ½ tsp salt
115g / 4oz / ½ cup butter, softened
115g / 4oz / ½ cup margarine, softened
115g / 4oz / ½ cup light brown sugar
225g / 8oz / 1 cup granulated sugar
120ml / 4fl oz / ½ cup black treacle
1 egg

MAKES 36

1 Preheat the oven to 160°C/325°F/Gas 3. Line and grease 2–3 baking sheets. Sift the flour, spices, baking powder and salt together three times.

2 Cream the butter and margarine, brown sugar and half of the granulated sugar until fluffy. Beat in the treacle, egg and flour. Chill to firm up.

3 Place the remaining granulated sugar in a shallow dish. Roll tablespoonfuls of the dough into balls, then roll the balls in the sugar to coat them well.

4 Place the balls 5cm/2in apart on the prepared sheets and flatten slightly. Bake for 12–15 minutes, until golden around the edges but soft in the middle. Leave for 5 minutes before cooling on a rack.

VARIATION
To make Gingerbread Men, increase the flour by 25g / 1oz / ¼ cup. Roll out the dough and cut out shapes. Bake and ice.

Pepper-Spice Biscuits

INGREDIENTS

150g/5oz/1¼ cups plain flour
115g/4oz/½ cup cornflour
10ml/2 tsp baking powder
2.5ml/½ tsp ground cardamom
2.5ml/½ tsp ground cinnamon
2.5ml/½ tsp grated nutmeg
2.5ml/½ tsp ground ginger
2.5ml/½ tsp ground allspice
2.5ml/½ tsp salt
2.5ml/½ tsp ground black pepper
225g/8oz/1 cup butter or margarine,
softened
115g/4oz/½ cup soft light
brown sugar
2.5ml/½ tsp vanilla essence
5ml/1 tsp finely grated lemon rind
50ml/2fl oz/¼ cup whipping cream
75g/3oz/¾ cup ground almonds

MAKES 48

1 Preheat the oven to 180°C/350°F/Gas 4. Sift the flour, cornflour, baking powder, spices, salt and ground pepper into a bowl. Set aside.

2 With a mixer or in a food processor, cream the butter or margarine and brown sugar together until light and fluffy. Beat in the vanilla and lemon rind.

3 With the mixer on low speed, add the spicy flour mixture alternately with the cream, beginning and ending with flour. Stir in the ground almonds.

4 Shape 2cm/¾in balls from the dough and place 2.5cm/1in apart on ungreased baking sheets. Bake for 15–20 minutes. Transfer to a wire rack to cool.

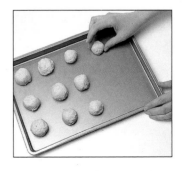

Cardamom & Saffron Tea Loaf

INGREDIENTS

good pinch of saffron strands
750ml/ 1¼ pints/ 3 cups lukewarm milk
25g/ 1oz/ 2 tbsp butter
900g/ 2lb/ 8 cups strong plain flour
2 sachets easy-blend dried yeast
45ml/ 3 tbsp caster sugar
6 cardamom pods, split open and seeds extracted
115g/ 4oz/ ⅔ cup raisins
30ml/ 2 tbsp clear honey, plus extra
for brushing
1 egg, beaten

SERVES 10–12

1 Crush the saffron into a cup containing a little of the warm milk and leave to infuse for 5 minutes.

2 Rub the butter into the flour then mix in the yeast, the sugar and the cardamom seeds (these may need rubbing to get them apart). Stir in the raisins.

3 Beat all of the remaining milk with the honey and egg, then mix this into the flour mixture with the saffron milk. Stir well until a firm dough is formed (you may not need all the milk: this will depend on the flour). Turn out the dough and knead it on a lightly floured board for 5 minutes.

4 Return the dough to the mixing bowl, cover with oiled clear film and leave in a warm place until doubled in size – this could take from 1–3 hours, depending on the ambient temperature.

5 Grease a 1kg/2¼lb loaf tin. Turn the dough out on to a floured board again, punch it down, knead for 3 minutes then shape it into a fat roll and fit it into the loaf tin.

6 Cover with a sheet of lightly oiled clear film and stand in a warm place until the dough begins to rise again. Preheat the oven to 200°C/400°F/Gas 6.

7 Bake the loaf for 25 minutes until golden brown and firm on top. Turn out of the tin and place on a wire rack. As the loaf cools brush the top with honey. Slice the tea loaf when cold.

Pumpkin Spice Bread

INGREDIENTS

10ml/2 tsp ground cinnamon
5ml/1 tsp ground ginger
5ml/1 tsp ground allspice
1.5ml/¼ tsp ground cloves
550g/1lb 6oz/5½ cups plain flour
5ml/1 tsp salt
2 sachets of easy-blend dried yeast
250g/9oz/generous 1 cup caster sugar
250ml/8fl oz/1 cup cooked or
canned pumpkin
115g/4oz/½ cup butter, melted
120ml/4fl oz/½ cup hand-hot milk
250ml/8fl oz/1 cup hand-hot water
50g/2oz/½ cup pecan nuts, finely chopped

MAKES 1 LOAF

1 Mix the spices together. Put 10ml/2 tsp of the spice mix in a mixing bowl. Add the flour, salt, yeast and 115g/4oz/½ cup of the sugar. Mash the pumpkin with 45ml/3 tbsp of the butter and all the milk. Add this to the flour mixture with enough of the water to make a dough. Knead on a floured surface until smooth. Return the dough to the clean bowl, cover and leave to rise in a warm place for about 1½ hours, or until doubled in bulk.

2 Punch the dough down and knead it briefly, then divide it into three equal pieces. Roll each piece into a 46cm/18in long rope. Cut each rope into 18 equal pieces, then roll each piece into a ball.

3 Grease a 25cm/10in ring or tube tin. Stir the remaining sugar into the remaining spice mixture. Roll each ball in turn in the remaining melted butter, then in the sugar and spice mixture.

4 Arrange all the dough balls in the prepared tin in staggered rows, in more than one layer, if necessary. Sprinkle the balls with the chopped nuts as you go.

5 Preheat the oven to 180°C/350°F/Gas 4. Cover the tin and stand in a warm place until the dough begins to rise again, then bake for 55 minutes. Cool in the tin for 20 minutes, then turn out on to a wire rack. Serve the bread warm.

Index